Spot the Mistake

Bible Story coloring book

Book 2

Bible Stories
Illustrated by *Andy Robb*

How to use this book

1. See how many deliberate mistakes you can find in each picture. You will find some very funny mistakes. You will also find some things, such as wrist-watches, that had not been invented in Bible times. You may want to circle the mistakes you find. Some of the mistakes are quite difficult to spot.

When you have finished, you can look up the answers at the back of the book. (Don't look until then!)

2. See if you can discover the answer to the question under the picture. It will help if you read the story in the Bible. (The verses you need to read are given.)

3. On every page a little mouse is hiding. See if you can find the mouse on each page.

4. Finally, you can color in the picture with crayons, colored pencils or felt-tips.

Copyright © 2001 Angus Hudson Ltd/Tim Dowley & Peter Wyart trading as Three's Company
ISBN 0 8254 7209 1
Published in the USA by Candle Books 2001
Distributed by: Kregel Publications, PO Box 2607 Grand Rapids, Michigan 49501

CANDLE BOOKS
GRAND RAPIDS, MICHIGAN

Worldwide coedition organised and produced by
Angus Hudson Ltd, London
Tel +44 208 959 3668
Fax +44 208 959 3678
E-m: coed@angushudson.com
Printed in England

Adam gives names to the different animals and birds.
Who told Adam to give names to all the animals and birds?
Read Genesis 2:19–20.

Noah puts the animals into the ark which he had just built.
How many of each kind of creature went into the ark?
You can read this story in your Bible. Read Genesis 6:9–22.

A tall tower is built which was meant to reach the sky.
What was the name of the tower?
This story is in Genesis 11:1–9.

Abram and his family leave their own country.
How old was Abram, later called Abraham, when he left his home?
You can read about this in Genesis 12:1–9.

Jacob has an amazing dream.
Who were going up and down a staircase in Jacob's dream?
You can read this story in your Bible. Read Genesis 28:10–19.

Joseph puts on his new, richly decorated, coat.
Who made Joseph's coat?
Read Genesis 37:1–11.

Joseph is sold as a slave.
Which brother tried to stop Joseph from being sold?
You can read this story in your Bible. Read Genesis 37:12–37.

Joseph had been put in prison, most unfairly.
Why did Pharaoh tell Joseph about his dream?
You can read about this in Genesis 40:1 – 41:40.

The baby Moses is hidden among the reeds.
Why was Moses put into the water like this?
This story is in Exodus 2:1–10.

The plague of frogs invades Pharaoh's palace.
Who is standing next to Moses in the picture?
You can read about this in Exodus 8:1–15.

Moses leads the people of Israel safely through the Red Sea.
Who were chasing after the people of Israel in their chariots?
You can read this story in your Bible. Read Exodus 14:1–22.

The people of Israel bow down in worship to the golden calf they had made.
Where did the people obtain the gold from to make their golden calf?
Read Exodus 32:1–35.

The spies return from exploring the land of Canaan.
What fruit did the spies bring back with them to show how good the land was?
You can read this story in your Bible. Read Numbers 13:1–33.

The people of Israel march around the walls of Jericho.
For how many days did they march around Jericho?
This story is in Joshua 5:13 – 6:20.

This lion attacked Samson, but Samson managed to kill it.
What made their home in the dead lion?
This story is in Judges 14:1–20.

16

Ruth collects the leftover grain in Boaz' field.
Do you know the happy ending to this story?
You can read about this in Ruth 2:1–23.

17

Hannah gives her son Samuel to serve the Lord in the temple.
What was the first thing Hannah did after she gave Samuel to serve in the temple?
This story is in 1 Samuel 1:21 – 2:11.

The shepherd boy David meets the Philistine giant.
What is the giant's name?
You can read this story in your Bible. Read 1 Samuel 17.

19

King Saul asked David to play him some music to soothe his troubled spirit.
The story says that some invisible person was with David. Who was this?
You can read this story in your Bible. Read 1 Samuel 16:14–23.

20

The queen of Sheba visits king Solomon in Jerusalem.
What presents did the queen of Sheba give to king Solomon?
You can read about this in 1 Kings 10:1–13.

The prophet Elijah is fed by ravens.
What did the ravens feed Elijah on? How many times a day did they come?
You can read this story in your Bible. Read 1 Kings 17:1–6.

Queen Esther has come to ask a favor of the king.
Esther invited the king to a banquet, with one other person. Who was he?
This story is in Esther 5 – 7.

Did you find these deliberate mistakes?

2. Naming Day in Eden: Tusk missing, buffalo horn, white zebra, deer ears missing, butterfly pattern, flying fish, tee-shirt, upside-down cloud, carpet on waterfall, lion's leg missing.

3. Noah and the Ark: Rabbit tail, feet missing, stripy giraffe, camel three humps, square window, funnel, anchor upside down, raining, pencil, crocodile going backwards.

4. The Tower of Babel: Missing rope, one shoe, ice cream, man sideways, cement mixer, ladder in mid-air, ladder horizontal, spoon, Eiffel Tower.

5. Abraham leaves Ur: Umbrella, missing foot, camel with extra leg, strawberry, giraffe, suitcase, woman going wrong way, leaves on staff, watch, Ur sign.

6. Jacob's dream: Pillow, foot missing, eyes open, angel going wrong way, mountain (instead of ladder), alarm clock, two moons, fish, owl upside down, church.

7. Jacob and his coat: Mirror reflection, mum giving coat, 'We love Joe', pig's head on sheep, tea pot, 'Sold' tag, window in sky, pleased brother, tie.

8. Joseph sold as a slave: Joseph wet, two colored coats, sunglasses, caravan, Gilead sign, ten shekels, rubber boot, boat, two suns, peaked cap.

9. Joseph explains Pharaoh's dream: Fat corn eating thin corn, sheep, cakes, Joseph still in prison, baker present, 'No idea', fish in window, six cows, cow upside down, chain missing, drink can.

10. Moses in bulrushes: Brother, Teddy bear, wooden crib, bulrush upside down, swimsuit, fisherman, chimney, starfish, sandal straps, snorkel.

11. Moses pleads with Pharaoh: Garden chair, flippers, fishing rod, Aaron's hand missing, Moses' coat, magicians making dogs, wall lamps, fish, sideways window, Frenchman.

12. Crossing the Red Sea: Camel walking backwards, fish with legs, Moses wading in water, palm tree, Dead Sea sign, double-headed staff, rubber ring, tank, long pants, stripes on road.

13. The golden calf: Sheep, worshiper wrong way, legs in air, extra arm, Moses happy, earrings still worn, worshiper floating, plane, watch, pipe.

14. The two spies return with grapes: Grapes missing, spear head upside down, sword floating, spy's sleeve missing, three spies, upside-down tree, upside-down bird, ice cream on head, high rise buildings, pencil.

15. Marching around Jericho: Flute, peaked hat, cross-hatch pattern on Ark, angel missing, soldier facing wrong way, high rise building, sunshade, upside-down building, sideways bricks, sleeve pattern, chefs hat.

16. Samson and the lion: Uses dagger instead of hand, butterflies, tiger, sandal strap, short-eared rabbit, light bulb, spotty-legged tiger, upside-down bush, two-headed tree, Samson bald.

17. Ruth gleans in Boaz' field: Bulrushes, drinks carton, 'Boz's Field' sign, Boaz' feet missing, Boaz sleeve pattern, teepee, slippers, fork missing, combine harvester, door upside down.

18. Hannah gives Samuel to the Temple: Samuel a bearded teenager, leg of jeans, goat lead, goat, bunch of flowers, fire tracks, Temple steps missing, clock, suitcase, sandal missing.

19. David and Goliath: Airplane, 'Gordon', bunch of flowers, Christmas tree, soldier facing wrong way, upside-down cloud, fishing rod, David afraid, wristwatch, arrow.

20. David plays for Saul: Guitar, guitar strings missing, shoe missing, Saul disliking music, sofa, sofa leg, pool cue, rug tassels missing, penguin, painting upside down, mail slot in door.

21. The queen of Sheba visits Solomon: Maidservant's earrings, bananas, leopard's spots, Solomon with three arms, giraffe's head, lady with moustache, low sun, small palm tree, television, leopard's head.

22. Elijah is fed by ravens: Duck, sandwich, duck's foot wrong, raining, upside-down raven, ski resort, raven's tail, other man, fish flying.

23. Queen Esther: Baseball bat, shoe missing, sneakers, upside-down jar, border pattern changes, apple, pencil, reading glasses, plug, floor tile.